SECOND EMPIRE

RICHIE HOFMANN

SECOND EMPIRE

RICHIE HOFMANN

Alice James Books
FARMINGTON, MAINE
www.alicejamesbooks.org

10 9 8 7 6 5 4 3 2 1

Alice James Books are published by Alice James Poetry Cooperative, Inc., an affiliate of the University of Maine at Farmington.

Alice James Books
114 Prescott Street
Farmington, ME 04938
www.alicejamesbooks.org

Library of Congress Cataloging-in-Publication Data

Hofmann, Richie, 1987-
  Second empire / Richie Hofmann.
    pages cm
  Includes bibliographical references.
  ISBN 978-1-938584-16-9
  I. Title.
  PS3608.O4798A6 2015
  811'.6--dc23

                    2015005082

Alice James Books gratefully acknowledges support from individual donors, private foundations, the University of Maine at Farmington, and the National Endowment for the Arts.

ART WORKS.
arts.gov

Contributions for the production of *Second Empire* made by: Debra Ann Hiton.

Cover Art: Fernando Vicente – Serie Atlas – Grito, www.fernandovicente.es

Contents

✳

SEA INTERLUDE: STORM 33

III

✳

Acknowledgments

The author wishes to thank the editors of the following publications:

32 Poems: "Bright Walls" (as "Untitled"), "Fly"

The Adroit Journal: "Midwinter"

The Common: "The Harbor"

Cosmonauts Avenue: "The Gates"

Denver Quarterly: "Antique Book" (as "Song")

Devil's Lake: "Scene from *Caravaggio*"

FIELD: "Imperium," "Abendlied"

Gulf Coast: "Description," "The Surround," "Gatekeeper"

Harvard Divinity Bulletin: "Capriccio"

Indiana Review: "Sea Interlude: Storm"

Lambda Literary Review: "At the Palais Garnier," "Egyptian Cotton"

Maggy: "Purple"

The Massachusetts Review: "Amor Vincit Omnia"

The Missouri Review: "Sea Interlude: Dawn," "Sea Interlude: Passacaglia," "Sea Interlude: Moonlight"

The New Criterion: "Illustration from *Parsifal*," "Mirror"

New England Review: "Night Ferry"

The New Republic: "October 29, 2012"

The New Yorker: "Idyll"

The Paris-American: "Allegory"

Ploughshares: "After"

Poetry: "Fresco," "Keys to the City," "Imperial City"

Poetry Northwest: "The Ships"

Shenandoah: "Braying"

The Southern Review: "Egyptian Bowl with Figs"

Southwest Review: "First Night in Stonington"

Tin House Online: "Second Empire"

The Yale Review: "Three Cranes"

"Fresco" was reprinted in *T: The New York Times Style Magazine*.

"Braying" was reprinted on Poetry Daily.

"Midwinter" was reprinted on Best of the Net 2014.

"After" was reprinted in *Best New Poets 2014*, edited by Dorianne Laux and Jazzy Danziger.

✻

For generous financial and artistic support, the author thanks the Poetry Foundation, Emory University, Johns Hopkins University, the James Merrill House, the New York State Summer Writers Institute at Skidmore College, West Chester University Poetry Conference, the Sewanee Writers' Conference, Bread Loaf Writers' Conference, and the Kenyon Review Writers Workshop. For encouragement, thank you to Natasha Trethewey, Mary Jo Salter, Emily Leithauser, Jacques J. Rancourt, Tarfia Faizullah, Lisa Hiton, and especially Kara van de Graaf. Thank you, Ryan Hagerty. Thank you, family.

This book is for Ryan.

SECOND EMPIRE

RICHIE HOFMANN

Sea Interlude: Dawn

Smoke-green mist leans into the rocks,
where fishermen whistle and mend their nets,
practicing rituals of brotherhood
before the luster of sky and sun,
which flashes against the pale horizon
with the oily turbulence of a swarm
of herring. Above, the familiar gulls
shriek the news of the world.
The ocean gurgles a dead language.
Standing at the water's edge, I watch myself
loosen into a brief, exquisite blur,
like Antinoüs, nearly naked in the cold,
in the morning gone adrift, turning away from love
toward what he knows, even then, is loss.

IDYLL

Cicadas bury themselves in small mouths
of the tree's hollow, lie against the bark-tongues like amulets,

though I am praying I might shake off this skin and be raised
from the ground again. I have nothing

to confess. I don't yet know that I possess
a body built for love. When the wind grazes

its way toward something colder,
you too will be changed. One life abrades

another, rough cloth, expostulation.
When I open my mouth, I am like an insect undressing itself.

THREE CRANES

1.

Wading low through marsh and grass,
quick and cautious, the crane, too,
            knows this: there is a freedom
in submitting to another. Cranes mate
for life. With necks outstretched,
      they take flight, a double arrow's stab
of silver, released and then gone.
            I have searched for nourishment
      in you, like a long, black beak
in the earth. How was I to know
what I would find there? Every night,
            we shrieked our presence to each other,
desire or grief lacquering us onto our lives
            like birds on a paneled screen.

2.

All winter long, the men built
another bridge, stacking slabs of metal
                and concrete near the barrier island
where we lived. I was worried we had fallen
from each other. Silent on the beach,
        we watched machines hoisted on and off
the earth. Standing one-legged in the marsh:
                a crane, all steel and orange light,
        binding the horizon.
What will become of us? I almost said.
Gulls wove in and out of the cables,
                shrieking up and down within the stacks,
in unison, I noticed, with our breath.
                It almost looked like a living thing.

3.

Lying on my stomach, reading
Crane's letters again, I felt a hand
                    behind me. Orange light pressed
the window. The hand that touched
my shoulder was yours ("I know now
        there is such a thing as indestructibility").
Your confessor, I listened for your breath
                    ("the cables enclosing us and pulling
        us upward"), but felt only the ceiling fan,
and traffic, somewhere, chafing against
a wet street. Then, your lips on my neck
                    ("I think the sea has thrown itself upon me
and been answered") before I closed the book
                    and turned my body under yours.

Egyptian Bowl with Figs

In the Egyptian gallery: dried fruit left in a bowl,
as if time and beetles and a dead king
had chewed around them,
                      picked the fig flesh
from his teeth, wiped clean his gaudy, painted lips,

before his body was brushed with resin, a ball
of linen lodged in his mouth, in his rectum;

before a hairless priest pulled the brain out through the nose
with a hook.
           So much history is painted in gold
on a golden door, the rest carried off in the floodplain,
or covered with earth, dropped in ceremonial jars

with the dead king's brain,
                    or into bowls of clay
and sycamore, like this one, which held me
for an hour, wondering how long a handful of figs
could nourish a man, myth-like.
                      But I am young.
My hair is the color of antique coins. No one I've loved
has died. How can I know or say what hunger is?

CAPRICCIO

From the leafy, walled-in courtyard beside the house,
where fountain water trickled

from a river-god's mouth
into the unseasonable heat of that afternoon, we watched

the heavy bees, clumsy in their flight, humming
against the bricks and orange tree blossoms.

Everywhere we walked, you would point out how the Japanese
  honeysuckle clung
to the walls and fences.

Each star-shaped flower scattered its breath into fragrance,
which the heavy air held around us,

until, as if no longer able,
a downpour,
all the aroma flushed away in the sky's own sighing—

IMPERIUM

As if yoked in a wooden beam, our bodies cross into the thrall
of the river,

whose name means red—hooves and sandals
with iron hobnails hammered

into the soles, one after the other
into the muddy water. We move at first like light on brass.

Now like a legion. Now a piece of the river
being crossed.

While resting in the dim-lit inner study,
I pulled a book down from the shelf—a dusty

old retelling of the opera, its once scarlet
cover crumbled now, faded to a claret's

brittle blood-purple. With care, I spread
a page, as one draws back the drapes,

not wanting to be seen. Inside, a youth, golden-
haired, marches undaunted toward his longed-

for future, the margin's blank. Beyond it, the treasure
he seeks. Walking at his back, two austerer

figures: a woman, who grips one dangling tress
of his tawny pelt as her lowered head rests

against his shoulder, and an old man, his beard
meager on a face pinched by hunger for bread,

who carries on his spindly shoulders the past
and in satchels at his side. He taps

the garland of fine-penciled earth with his tapered
staff, as if to stir the souls of those who predate

this moment—under the red dust, the veil
of aging paper, those people who no longer live.

First Night in Stonington

So rare in this country to pace the streets
of another century, to wander and survey
gray alleys, cobbled by colonists and pilgrims,
and crooked houses later built for fleets
of Portuguese fishermen, whose heirs, today,
received the bishop's yearly blessing: sailors' hymns
and holy water. In the town square, someone
has set a cannonball, the balding, black veneer
freckled with rust, on a tapered pillar embellished
with the date of its arrival, a battle won
by port-merchants and innkeepers' wives. All here:
these long-dead people's memories, cherished
and chiseled into iron.
                        In this apartment, too,
another story preserved in the black chair
where no one sits; in boxes stuffed with photographs,
loose buttons, and playing cards; the faded blue
of Japanese prints. A book, open like hands in prayer,
rustles when the window draws a breath.

FRESCO

I have come again to the perfumed city.
Houses with tiered porches, some decorated with shells.
You know from the windows that the houses
are from a different time. I am not
to blame for what changes, though sometimes
I have trouble sleeping.
Between the carriage houses,
there are little gardens separated by gates.
Lately, I have been thinking about the gates.
The one ornamented with the brass lion, I remember
it was warm to the touch
even in what passes here for winter.
But last night, when I closed my eyes,
it was not the lion that I pictured first.

SEA INTERLUDE: PASSACAGLIA

Pulling the rowboat into shallower water,
you wedged an oar into the rocks. I squinted
down at the fish, struggling to see them
like a memory in which only part
of a moment returns, the rest somehow unlit,
blank like a swath of tiles missing
from a Byzantine mosaic—a scar
that will not reflect another century's light.
Later, when the boat and your body
and the light have found their way,
what will there be for me? Will the scales,
elegant as hammered gold, shine through
the water? Or will I have lost them already,
fallen through my hands, every one?

ALLEGORY

As it was for the ancients, it would be for me: songs written down
in pictures. The one about the trees on fire

when I came upon them, and the grass flattened around me—
that was what I saw.
                       The trees are like a fresco,
I thought, insofar as they are gold and tell a story.

We always arrived late,
    sometimes in masks. You wore a sword
at your side. The heads that watched
    our little pageant were busts of the great composers
and not men lined up for the executions.
    The style was Second Empire,
but the Empire had already fallen
    by the time the façade was finished.
The casts changed seasonally
    like our lovers. I remember,
through black-lace fans, Hänsel & Gretel
    eating a garish cake in the darkness.
We covered our mouths
    when we laughed at the children trapped
in the house of sweets. We ate cake at intermission
    in order to stay awake.

SCENE FROM *CARAVAGGIO*

Meanwhile, the artist's hand
spreads black against black,

the rest of him offscreen, grinding
colors—divine wine for the lips, underside-

of-watercress for the skin—glancing back toward me,
as if I am in the picture.

Watching him, alone
in lived time, I feel anachronistic, like the fedora

he wears, the cigarette he holds
against his lips with two fingers.

The screen I watch is a canvas strewn
with nudity, with the taken-

down, everything happening all
too late. The artist paints an angel, posed

on a box with a quiver,
though in the glow of the film, I can see

he is only a model with props in a studio.
Artificial light

burns in the stillness,
chiaroscuro. The other half

veiled and equivocal, like the room
in which I myself am staged.

       In which the screen illuminates
my mouth and forehead and eyes.

In which the difference between an angel
and a boy with wings is real.

MIRROR

You'd expect a certain view from such a mirror—
clearer
than one that hangs in the entry and decays.
I gaze
past my reflection toward other things:
bat wings,
burnt gold upon blue, which decorate the wall
and all
those objects collected from travels, now seen
between
its great, gold frame, diminished with age:
a stage
where, still, the supernatural corps de ballet
displays
its masquerade in the reflected light.
At night,
I thought I'd see the faces of the dead.
Instead,
the faces of the ghosted silver sea
saw me.

Antique Book

The sky was crazed with swallows.
We walked in the frozen grass
of your new city, I was gauzed with sleep.

Trees shook down their gaudy nests.
The ceramic pots were caparisoned with snow.
I was jealous of the river,

how the light broke it, of the skein
of windows where we saw ourselves.
Where we walked, the ice cracked

like an antique book, opening
and closing. The leaves
beneath it were the marbled pages.

DESCRIPTION

Where you were, everything was becoming ice.
The paved courtyard, the windows looking out onto it.
You traveled back and forth between buildings on a bus,
passing trees and umbrellas
inverted in the wind. You moved back and forth.
I was elsewhere, in a small studio
painted white so many times the walls were thick with it.
Once a poet told me, *Your eyes are whores.*
Once description was all I thought I needed
to bridge things. And snow shawled the branches.
And you took the keys from your pocket. And snow feathered the grass
which was mine to remember and forget.

Amor Vincit Omnia

Some nights, we lived that way: like a horse
carrying his rider, unseen, into a village—
There was nothing to do there but memorize
each other.
        Returning, we smelled of where we'd been:
the markets, the metal troughs, the trees,
the hands that touched our heads.

Nothing changes at the seaside house.
You wait out this tempest in the Windsor chair, away from the windows.
There are books for your eyes:

one about Pound as a young man, one with photographs
of glaciers. For your hands:
frozen dough thawing. Towels in the dryer.

There is music; a crate of CDs you purchased
when you were younger, when you resisted solitude by listening
to massive collaborations:

32 violins, 6 French Horns, 8 double basses, a piccolo.
The one on top is Mahler's fifth,
conducted by Leonard Bernstein, who was buried

with that score across his heart. Someone extinguishes
the lamps along the beach. Mahler drowns out
the weather against the roof.

Didn't rain choke the animal throats
of the cathedral   sputter
against the roofs of the city   didn't the flight
of stairs rise up above the cobbled street
didn't the key clamor
in the lock   flood
the vestibule with clattering   didn't we climb
the second flight
toward the miniature Allegory
painted on the ceiling
and touch the flat-faced girls
winged   part animal
who did not flinch and did not scamper

SEA INTERLUDE: STORM

Where the sky, Chinese red, dropped
its rawboned chin to the sea, that darkness
opened, hollow as an empty boat:
it could not hold itself; nor the seabirds,
where they fled or resisted,
tossed like heavy, black stones toward the shore.
With the fuss and tumult of a thousand feathers
fanning open, the surge, black-throated,
drank of itself, like a ritual, then folded
its wet wings across the shoals and sandbanks,
sated at last as from self-love. That night, I clung
like a feeding gull to the sureness of flesh:
a man's chin bristled against my stomach
like the breakers' dim retreat on sand.

BRIGHT WALLS

It was not penitence I sought, standing outside
the bedroom in the old apartment

where you had spent the night alone.
To bend, to kneel before some greater force—

that was no longer what I wished.
Clouds blew in from the coast, and I felt

the sun abandoning the window behind me,
making the bright walls suddenly colorless,

obscuring everything, for a moment,
that I wanted. When I finally entered,

I saw you still asleep—a wet strand
of hair tucked behind your ear, the husk

of your body—and lingered there for a minute,
before walking upstairs to shut the windows.

EROTIC ARCHIVE

We sleep in his bed

among his silent books.

Though I never knew him,

I've spent my life thinking it's his ghost

I belong to.

        We pass his books

between us. We read inscriptions

meant for him. We record them

dutifully. Remembering

the blue room of an evening,

I look past the window

the light changes through,

                past the boats

with their tied-up sails and canvas covers.

The window shows

the sea as unattainable

        and distant as art,

our lovers far away.

THE HARBOR

Afterwards everything whitened
like paper or breath—
The room was suddenly anchored to itself,
the chains stopped groaning.
I knew I could not leave with you.
The sea outside was like the sea
on the map. A sea-god was blowing
into a crosshatched arc of sails.

PURPLE

From the Phoenicians, they learned to extract
the color from shells.
When their dogs ate sea snails along the coast,
their dogteeth were dyed purple—that's how the Phoenicians knew.

To darken it,
the Romans added black, which came from soot, from scorched wood,
which abounded, one imagines, in an empire.

The Ships

from an inscription of Augustus

"All the Germans
> of that territory
sought by envoys
> my friendship

The far reaches
> of what any Roman had ever seen
opened to me
> the mouth

> of the Rhine   the water
swallowing the gold-
> colored hulls
What gods

> would I find in the forests
in the riverbanks
> scattered
with precious stones

I sailed my ships
> on the sea   dark
and full of meaning
> When

            our sails first caught
the wind
            of the Cimbri   it was rough
as their language

I watched
            their shirtless oarsmen
maneuvering
            the oars

I watched the ships
            running their fingers
through the water
            of the Roman people"

BRAYING

Now is the time we hear them coming back,
when the first sunlight drops to the field
like an animal being born, slick and shivering
where it falls. Their hooves grind against the earth,
wheat is pounded in a mortar
with a pestle, freed from its husks and impurities.
What wickedness clings to me, it sticks
to the last. I will keep my mouth with a bridle.

FLY

What the richest man in Rome feared most of all,
Pliny tells us, was losing his sight. The man wore Greek charms
around his neck in order to prevent it. He carried a living fly
in a white cloth that he might keep seeing.
Perhaps he thought the fly's many eyes were a blessing.
Apologizing, devising elaborate rituals—what
will I carry? I have been counting ways
of keeping you.

Second Empire

The water, for once,
unmetaphysical. Stepping over
the stones, you pulling

your shirt over your shoulders.
The flesh-and-
blood that constitutes you

could have been anything and yet

appears before me
as your body. Wading out again,

I am a little white omnivore

in the black water,
inhaling avidly
the absence of shame.

We lie on our backs
with our underwear on.

The soul is an aristocrat.

It disdains the body,
staring through the water
at the suggestion of our human forms.

NIGHT FERRY

I. DEATH IN VENICE

Everywhere the city looks over my shoulder.
The air grows colder

and sticks to wet stones, the old houses rescued
from the rising water, even the covered boat where I take refuge

from the wind, still it tousles the pages
of my guidebook. The ferry disengages

from the docks, and I am far away. The Adriatic salts
the undersides of boats

as they depart from the city, fade.
I lean and see what is made

in their wake. I know I will not find my dissolution
here in this city of water and stone,

where I'm a hierophant
to the past. They enchant

me, these things. I always knew
they'd make the veil I'd glimpse things through.

Tonight, distantly, the cold air
comes off the square,

where all those people, bundled in winter coats,
line up to buy tickets for the boats.

Everywhere the city disguises
them from each other. The black ferry moves. The water rises

in the dark.
The people disembark.

II. THE MARRIAGE OF THE SEA

The city remembered nothing of what I dreamed.
Only how strange it seemed

from the water when the Doge's hand,
or his black glove, opened,

and he released the ring
to wed the Adriatic, and the ring

settled twice:
first, on the lagoon's surface,

which represented, I thought,
the comfort

of the living moment, and which yielded to the ring; and, later,
in the earth beneath the water,

which was fierce
as history, and which yielded to it also, after many years,

and found stasis in the past,
which was its rest,

not in the luster
of ceremonies, but in the darkness which comes after.

III. SELF-PORTRAIT IN VENETIAN MASK

The mask with a long, sharp beak
I found, an antique

in a store of relics, displayed
on the wall. The mask I tried on. Like a shade,

it kept me from my life. *You, too, have wished*
for something else, you have vanished

almost fully, the mask said, as if a mask critiquing
itself could convince me it was not my own mouth speaking.

IV. SERENITY

The city cleaved things: together
and apart: a bridge restrained one ancient house from another:

the whole city was reflected below
the city: the bridge where they hanged prisoners: the tableau

of bodies held suspended
as on a frieze, splendid

with color and movement: thousands
of bits of glass: small islands

of gold and purple and bronze glued
into images: a pagan nude

with a feather: halos in concentric rings: the rudder
cut its dark path through the water,

pushing wake to either side, as if sorting testimonies of love
from jealousy: from above,

it must have looked like the black canal was rent
apart, halved, no matter where I went.

SEA INTERLUDE: MOONLIGHT

Nearly asleep, I thought of the wrecked
fishing ship—its hull, scuffed and split
open, scraped clean of its entrails
by the rusty brine that now pools
around the timbers, scouring the sand.
Searching for you in the hollow cage
of its body, the ribs of copper and wood
which once held men, I sensed a trembling,
as from a distant wharf, the dull thunder
of a body cast back into another
like a beach sea-worn to obedience:
my hunger, fallen into air from the mouth
of language; and the moonlight stiffening
around it like a mollusk's silver shell.

The Surround

That summer I was looking for an antidote
to art. I woke up early and spent
mornings swimming, wading out
with tiny piping plovers, whose nests
along the strip of beach had been roped off
with netting as protected land.
I wanted lust to exhaust itself. I wanted
the alchemy of someone else
to rise in me. Sitting with you on the terrace,
I scarcely noticed. Bats tacked blackness
to the sky, erotic and detached
as Japanese tattoos. One by one, stars broke
sharply into the harbor
like silver extracted from lead in a bowl.

ABENDLIED

All the animals in the city: blood
in a butcher's window. Beneath
a butcher's stoop. A white parrot
in an opera lover's bedroom:
keeping watch, telling. I hear them all.
Even a family crest above an entrance
studded with bees. Even a lion
with a ring in his mouth. Even the lips
troubled with knocking.

MIDWINTER

Wearing Wellington boots, we followed the retriever
along the perimeter of the property.

Just that morning a man and his son
had brought in firewood from the fallen tree.

Through barberry: a small clearing
in the woods, hollow like the inside of a cello.

I walked around a tree stump, like Mustardseed.
After sunset, we looked through a square window

into the stark cabin where Jean writes.
In a bubble in the antique glass, the sky swirled—

reflected like a sequin, like summer even,
though it was New Years Day, and the world

was dusky, and the dog, the house, the woods, the books—
they weren't even ours.

The Gates

The crystal doorknob coils
back. Light
shifts into
a new pattern

on the ceiling, as it did
from time
to time, when
the swallows left

the tree outside the window,
when there was a tree—
How else
can I describe your leaving,

farfetched
as it seems?

GATEKEEPER

In another time, the choice
might have been depicted as two gates:

Open the one, and it is winter.
Snow covers the cobblestones, the spires,
the December markets shrill
with lettuces. Snow covers the butcher's stoop,
the little chapel. The iron gates at the far edge of the city, of sleep—
I thought I saw you there.

Open the other, and it is winter.
I can tell because the lion's mouth is filled with snow.
In a room, my lover presses a photograph of the city
against glass, and fastens
the back of the frame, which has hinges also, and opens
and closes.

Egyptian Cotton

Once nothing separated us but the gossamer
of sheets—white and gauzy in the summer, when a world
of heat blew in, inflating
the curtains into the room that was his
and mine, when no one else was there—
nothing between the body, whose hot-bloodedness,
whose frailty I had come to know
the duration of my life,
                         and the body
he drank cool water with, the body he salted, mile after mile
along the coast, fucked me with, with which
he told me what troubled him
                         —the two of us in our bed
of Egyptian cotton.
The sea reflected us, our human emotions.
Then the sea refused us, like the sea.

After

When the sun broke up the thunderheads,
and dissonance was consigned
to its proper place, the world was at once foreign
and known to me. That was shame
leaving the body. I had lived my life
from small relief to small relief, like a boy pulling a thorn
from his foot. Wet and glistening,
twisting toward light, everything seemed
recognizable again: a pheasant lazily dragging
his plume; the cherries dark and shining
on the trellis; moths hovering cotton-like
over an empty bowl; even myself,
where I reclined against an orange wall,
hopeful and indifferent, like an inscription on a door.

Imperial City

From the outset I hated the city of my ancestors.
I was fearful I'd be put in the dungeon below
the cathedral. The best example of the Romanesque
a guide was saying in German   in English   in French
where are buried eight German kings   four queens
twenty-three bishops   four Holy Roman Emperors
all of whom used this bishopric on the river as the seat
of the kingdom. On the old gate at one end a clock
told an ancient form of time. I sulked along behind
my parents as the guide gave facts about the war
with the Saracens   about the place where the Jews bathed
about the child like me whose father the Peaceful
having already produced an heir by his first marriage
could marry   for love.

Notes

The four "Sea Interludes" take their titles from Benjamin Britten's interludes from his opera, *Peter Grimes*.

"Three Cranes": The quoted passages in section 3 are taken from Hart Crane's letter to Waldo Frank, dated April 21, 1924, reprinted in *O My Land, My Friends: the Selected Letters of Hart Crane*, edited by Langdon Hammer and Brom Weber.

"Illustration from *Parsifal*": See Willy Pogány's illustrations in the E. W. Rolleston translation of Wagner's *Parsifal* published in 1912. This poem is for J. D. McClatchy.

"Scene from *Caravaggio*": Derek Jarman's.

"Erotic Archive": The italicized line is from James Merrill's *Mirabell: Books of Number.*

"The Ships": From the *Res Gestae Divi Augusti* ("The Deeds of Divine Augustus"), a funerary inscription written for Augustus' death in A.D. 14.

"Braying": See Psalm 39 and Proverbs 27.

"Second Empire": The line "inhaling avidly the absence..." translates a line from Alda Merini's poem "Apro la sigaretta."

"Night Ferry": Some language in this poem was suggested by Myfanwy Piper's libretto for Benjamin Britten's opera version of *Death in Venice*.

"Midwinter": This poem is for Emily Leithauser.

Book Benefactors

Alice James Books wishes to thank the following individuals who generously contributed toward the publication of *Second Empire*:

Kazim Ali
Lynn & Jeff Callahan
Elizabeth Hagerty
Christine Hofmann
Linda Hofmann
Cynthia Vena

For more information about AJB's book benefactor program, contact us via phone or email, or visit alicejamesbooks.org to see a list of forthcoming titles.

Recent Titles from Alice James Books

Alice James Books has been publishing poetry since 1973. The press was founded in Boston, Massachusetts as a cooperative wherein authors performed the day-to-day undertakings of the press. This collaborative element remains viable even today, as authors who publish with the press are also invited to become members of the editorial board and participate in editorial decisions at the press. The editorial board selects manuscripts for publication via the press's annual, national competition, the Alice James Award. Alice James Books seeks to support women writers and was named for Alice James, sister to William and Henry, whose extraordinary gift for writing went unrecognized during her lifetime.

Designed by Mary Austin Speaker